ΨLivi

2024-2025

Prayer Journal

This journal belongs to:

_____

© 2024 Novalis Publishing Inc.

Cover: Jamie Wyatt
Interior design and layout: Jessica Llewellyn

Published in Canada by Novalis

Publishing Office
1 Eglinton Ave East, Suite 800
Toronto, Ontario, Canada
M4P 3A1

Head Office
4475 Frontenac Street
Montréal, Québec, Canada
H2H 2S2

www.novalis.ca

ISBN (for Canada):
978-2-89830-247-3

Published in the United States by Bayard, Inc.

500 Salisbury St.
Worcester, MA 01609

www.livingwithchrist.us

ISBN (for USA):
978-1-62785-803-8

Cataloguing in Publication is available from Library and Archives Canada.

Printed in Canada.

All rights reserved. No part of this publication may be reproduced, stored in a retrieval system, or transmitted in any form, or by any means, electronic, mechanical, photocopying, recording, or otherwise, without the written permission of the publisher.

We acknowledge the support of the Government of Canada.

5   4   3   2   1   19   18   17   16   15

*The best guide you can find
to the correct spiritual path
is the serious study of the Bible.
There we can find rules for the conduct of our life
and, in the lives of the great figures,
living images of a life with God
whose actions we are encouraged to copy.*

— *St. Basil the Great*

Why journal?

SPIRITUAL JOURNALING IS a form of prayer. Far beyond recapping our life's events, the exercise of journaling helps us to express our spiritual life. Our written words capture our spiritual experiences, thoughts, struggles, victories – and essentially form a prayer through which we communicate to God what lies in our innermost self.

The exercise of spiritual journaling does not require us to be experienced in such a practice, nor are there any specific guidelines. When we journal, we need not worry about style or formalities. Just as in our regular prayers, Jesus wishes us to speak freely, simply, and honestly what is in our heart.

This journal provides a guideline to your prayer exercise in the **Responding to the Word** section each day, where you will find a question that is directly connected to the readings of the day. If this question is helpful, feel free to use it, but do not feel constrained by it.

Spiritual journaling will essentially enlarge our vision and lead to a greater understanding of our spiritual journey.

Prayer for the Help of the Holy Spirit

Come, Holy Spirit,
fill the hearts of your faithful
and kindle in them the fire of your love.
Send forth your Spirit
and they shall be created,
and you shall renew the face of the earth.
O God, who by the light of the Holy Spirit,
did instruct the hearts of the faithful,
grant that by the same Holy Spirit
we may be truly wise
and ever enjoy his consolations.
Through the same Christ Our Lord.
Amen.

SUNDAY DECEMBER 1

1st Sunday of Advent

I*F SOMEONE ASKED* what gives you hope in a world often marked by war, violence, poverty, and intolerance, how would you answer? As we enter this season of hope, does the world seem any more humane than when we gathered to celebrate the beginning of Advent last year?

In spite of staggering world problems, we take hope in the promise of rescue from Jeremiah: "I will cause a righteous Branch to spring up for David." Throughout the Hebrew scriptures, God promises and fulfills these promises. Those in bondage are led out of the desert of oppression. God hears the cry of the poor and sends prophets to serve as advocates on their behalf.

Jesus fulfills Jeremiah's prophecy of the "righteous Branch." In Luke, the coming of the Son of Man promises that even during human history's most fearful times we will not be left alone – instead, Jesus will rescue all who place their hope in him. His is a prodigal love that leaves no one behind. Perhaps the greatest hope is a heart open to change, to begin again on the road to conversion.

This Advent offers another opportunity to heal relationships, encourage those who have little hope, and build bridges in our communities. Our hope is strengthened by the realization that we are not alone, but continue the ministry of Jesus.

Sr. Judy Morris, OP

SUNDAY DECEMBER 1

People and Prayers to Remember this Week

Readings of the Day

Jeremiah 33.14-16
Psalm 25

1 Thessalonians 3.12 – 4.2
Luke 21.25-28, 34-36

Responding to the Word

God declares that now is the time for fulfilling promises. What promises do I most desire to be fulfilled?

Final Thoughts ...

Feasts this Week

December 3	**St Francis Xavier**
December 4	**St John Damascene**
December 6	**St Nicholas**
December 7	**St Ambrose**

SUNDAY DECEMBER 8

2nd Sunday of Advent

LATELY I'VE BEEN feeling that a lot of things are off track in the world. Despite our having enough food to feed the planet, millions are starving. Even in North America, a land of plenty, countless families increasingly rely on food banks. We know we need to care for the Earth, our common home, but we buy too much stuff and fill our world with garbage and pollution. Despite seeing the damage conflict causes, we think peace is out of our reach.

Baruch and John the Baptist speak of the Lord making the crooked straight and the rough ways smooth; this gives me hope that we can find some balance. John the Baptist invites the people of his day, and us, to turn back to God and prepare the way of the Lord – not only during Advent, but all year long.

As followers of Christ, we are meant to live in ways that make the crooked straight. Of course, it's not always easy. It means doing things differently. We may even need to spend some time in the wilderness – disconnected from social media, the Internet, malls, and TV – to adjust our attitudes and rediscover what's important. But when we do, we will truly understand that, as today's psalm tells us, "The Lord has done great things for us," and we will be "filled with joy."

Anne Louise Mahoney

SUNDAY DECEMBER 8

People and Prayers to Remember this Week

Readings of the Day

Baruch 5.1-9
Psalm 126

Philippians 1.3-6, 8-11
Luke 3.1-6

Responding to the Word

God levels the road so we can draw near to God more easily. How has God made my way easier than I thought it would be?

Final Thoughts ...

Feasts this Week

December 9	**Immaculate Conception of the Blessed Virgin Mary**
December 10	**Our Lady of Loreto**
December 11	**St Damasus I**
December 12	**Our Lady of Guadalupe**
December 13	**St Lucy**
December 14	**St John of the Cross**

MONDAY DECEMBER 9

Immaculate Conception of the Blessed Virgin Mary

AMONG THE CHRISTMAS cards you may have already received, you might find one with a beautiful picture of the Annunciation. And if you look at the picture again, you are likely to see a beautiful young Mary, eyes downcast, with a serious yet humble look on her face. She is a very holy person who has heard God's call and clearly said "Yes."

But wait. That picture doesn't tell the whole story. Mary's first response was not a clear and simple yes. Luke tells us that at first she was "much perplexed." Her second response was still not yes. Instead, she wanted a clarification. What could the words of God's messenger mean and how did they apply to her?

At the beginning of this famous story, Mary is confused, puzzled, and uncertain whether God's call can really be meant for her. Only after she has experienced and admitted her doubts, does she feel free to make her decision.

We shouldn't let the Christmas card image mislead us. When each of us receives God's personal call – as we surely do – Mary can be our model. We too can hesitate, feel uncertain and wonder what is expected of us, as we consider our response. May we respond with a clear and simple "Yes."

Patrick Gallagher

MONDAY DECEMBER 9

People and Prayers to Remember this Week

Readings of the Day

Genesis 3.9-15, 20
Psalm 98

Ephesians 1.3-6, 11-12
Luke 1.26-38

Responding to the Word

Mary's "yes" to God is unconditional and puts her completely at God's service. What conditions do I try to set for what God seems to be asking me to be or do?

Final Thoughts ...

SUNDAY DECEMBER 15

3rd Sunday of Advent

Rejoice! It is the word that best embodies the third Sunday of Advent. It's like a beautifully wrapped gift that we can't wait to open. We know we are getting close to Christmas and close to receiving a most wondrous gift: the birth of Christ. This expectation and the need to prepare ourselves for this wondrous event mark Advent. We are eager to celebrate an event that changed everything and gave all people new hope.

What is more joyous than a newborn… and yet, what is more vulnerable? It is in such poverty and vulnerability that Jesus comes. Advent is about preparing for Christ's coming. We must renew our commitment as Christians to reach out to others, especially the most vulnerable, and to let our "gentleness be known to everyone."

In the gospel, when people ask John the Baptist what they should do, he says whoever has two coats must share with someone who has none. If they have food to eat, they must ensure the hungry are fed.

As we prepare for Christ's coming, bear in mind that Jesus comes not as a great ruler in flowing robes of gold and silk. He comes as a vulnerable child who requires our concern, nurturing, and care.

Jack Panozzo

SUNDAY DECEMBER 15

People and Prayers to Remember this Week

Readings of the Day

Zephaniah 3.14-18a
Isaiah 12

Philippians 4.4-7
Luke 3.10-18

Responding to the Word

The crowds ask John what to do to change their lives. What should I do this week to change my life to be more like what Jesus wants?

Final Thoughts …

Feasts this Week

December 21   St Peter Canisius

SUNDAY DECEMBER 22

4th Sunday of Advent

As a mother, I remember well those first fleeting taps that signaled the kicks of my growing baby and knowing that one day, soon, the baby would arrive. After all the preparation and waiting, we would welcome an everyday miracle into a home that would perhaps never be truly ready enough.

This Advent, we hear once more how Elizabeth greeted Mary and we feel the Christ child move, already within us through the grace of baptism. Christ quickens within us in anticipation as we clean, shop, bake, write cards or emails, practice for the pageant, and wrap gifts. But sometimes we feel like the child is not leaping with joy but rather lagging a little. We miss loved ones and are burdened by imperfect relationships. We can feel that no matter how hard we work, something is lacking. It is so easy to become caught up in the material aspects of the season. We forget that all we need to do is be ready.

This Sunday, we are so close to the fulfillment of the promise contained in today's readings. What does fulfillment mean for us? For Elizabeth, it meant she was assured of God's blessing. This Christmas, let us, with Elizabeth, lay claim to that promise and may we all find some small moment to leap for joy.

Maureen Wicken

SUNDAY DECEMBER 22

People and Prayers to Remember this Week

Readings of the Day

Micah 5.2-5a (Canada)
Micah 5.1-4a (USA)
Psalm 80

Hebrews 10.5-10
Luke 1.39-45

Responding to the Word

Mary is blessed because she believed that what God promised would be fulfilled. Which of God's promises most inspires me with confidence?

Final Thoughts ...

Feasts this Week

December 23	St John of Kanty
December 25	Nativity of the Lord
December 26	St Stephen
December 27	St John
December 28	Holy Innocents

WEDNESDAY DECEMBER 25

Nativity of the Lord

CHRISTMAS IS ONE of those times when we can feel both the gift and the absence of belonging. The Christmas readings speak a word of hope and promise about where and to whom we belong.

We have our first experience of belonging in our family. Sometimes families are strong, and other times they are stretched to breaking. Throughout our lives, our circles of belonging fluctuate through all the changes we encounter (for instance, marriage, divorce, illness, births, deaths, relocation).

The Christmas night gospel begins by describing how Mary and Joseph set out for Bethlehem, the home of his ancestors, highlighting the importance of both family and place. John's gospel on Christmas day firmly places Jesus, the Word, both with God and among us. Both these gospels challenge us to shift our perception of belonging to another family – the family of God's children to whom God has appeared in the flesh, in Jesus. We are all children of God, members of God's family, and we are called to reach out to one another in this season of great joy.

Let us praise God for the wonderful gift of a Savior, Jesus, born to us this day and every day. Let us make our own the angels' song: "Glory to God in the highest heaven, and on earth peace among those whom God favors!"

Sr. Carmen Diston, IBVM

WEDNESDAY DECEMBER 25

People and Prayers to Remember this Week

Readings of the Day

Mass during the Night:
Isaiah 9.2-4, 6-7
Psalm 96
Titus 2.11-14
Luke 2.1-16

Mass at Dawn:
Isaiah 62.11-12
Psalm 97
Titus 3.4-7
Luke 2.15-20

Mass during the Day:
Isaiah 52.7-10
Psalm 98
Hebrews 1.1-6
John 1.1-18

Responding to the Word

Jesus is the finest revelation of who God is and what God wants for us. How can I pay closer attention to Jesus' example for my life?

Final Thoughts …

SUNDAY DECEMBER 29

Holy Family of Jesus, Mary and Joseph

The journey to Jerusalem for the Passover is difficult, often taking days of walking. The city is crowded, filled to the edges with people from all over the region and beyond. The air is thick with smoke and with the smell of burnt offering and blood. And of course, Roman soldiers keep a watchful eye.

Imagine losing your child in this city, searching frantically for three days and the joyful relief at finding him safe! Jesus' cheeky response on being found always takes me by surprise. Even at twelve, he is aware of his origin. But Mary, his mother, the life-giver, the courageous woman who said "yes," knows there is more in her son's destiny. She collects these moments and ponders as she did when the shepherds visited Bethlehem at Jesus' birth. She and Joseph, after all, are the first people to know Jesus' true nature and have the greatest hand in shaping him.

Their approach of patience, listening, and thoughtful meditation as they raise Jesus is a key touchstone that can guide us during our most difficult times. Like Mary, we too can benefit from this reflection on our own lives, listening for the messages from God to help us navigate our destinies.

Saskia Sivananthan

SUNDAY DECEMBER 29

People and Prayers to Remember this Week

Readings of the Day

1 Samuel 1.20-22, 24-28
Psalm 84

1 John 3.1-2, 21-24
Luke 2.41-52

Responding to the Word

As God's children, we are to be dedicated to God's ways. How might I offer myself in God's service today?

Final Thoughts …

Feasts this Week

December 31	**St Sylvester I**
January 1	**Mary, the Holy Mother of God**
January 2	**St Basil the Great & St Gregory Nazianzen**
January 3	**Most Holy Name of Jesus**
January 4	**St Elizabeth Ann Seton (USA)**

WEDNESDAY JANUARY 1
World Day of Peace

Mary, the Holy Mother of God

IN THE FIFTH century, Mary received the official title "Mother of God" or *Theotokos* (Greek for "bearer of God"). But let's go back to the beginning of the first century, as described in today's gospel.

Mary had just given birth in a cold and smelly stable. The only crib was an animal feeding trough. Could Mary even remember the angel Gabriel's words that she would bear a son whose kingdom would have no end? And what about her proclamation that God was great for having blessed her, a lowly young girl, with this privilege? Did she still mean it?

Mary could well have lost faith in God's promise, but she did not. When the shepherds arrived with their announcement of the angels' message that this baby was the Messiah, she was not amazed. She simply "treasured all these words and pondered them in her heart." For her, there was no contradiction between her child's identity and the poverty of the stable and of the shepherds who bore the good news that God's promise had been fulfilled.

It is through the humble that God's presence enters the world. Like Mary, we too are invited to be "bearers of God": humble enough to trust in God's promises, to treasure and ponder God's word in our hearts, and to actively assume the role of building the kingdom of peace.

Ferdinanda Van Gennip

WEDNESDAY JANUARY 1

People and Prayers to Remember this Week

Readings of the Day

Numbers 6.22-27
Psalm 67

Galatians 4.4-7
Luke 2.16-21

Responding to the Word

Mary is the model of our prayer, reflecting in her heart upon the meaning of Jesus' presence among us. How can I deepen my experience of his presence during the coming year?

Final Thoughts …

SUNDAY JANUARY 5

Epiphany of the Lord

Epiphania: A revelation, a proclamation, a broadcast. Such is the meaning of the feast of the Epiphany, usually understood as the revelation of the Incarnation to the world beyond the Chosen People, a revelation to the Gentiles.

It is a story full of the exotic: heavenly portents, mysterious wise men, precious gifts, dreams and visions, all leading the world to the astonishing mystery of God-made-flesh. The curious thing in this story is that these strange visitors from the East do not seem in the least dismayed by the discovery that this supposed king of the Jews is born in poverty. Undeterred by the humble circumstances, they pay him homage and offer their gifts.

This is an encounter replete with symbolism and meaning. What stands out is the fact that these wise men discovered the birth of the king by interpreting the signs they had observed. Not limited by presuppositions, false expectations, or jealousy, they could see the truth and accept it, where others could not.

Let us pray with grateful hearts for the wisdom to see Christ revealed in the world around us, even when that revelation challenges our preconceptions and invites us to find him where we least expect him.

Rev. Len Altilia, SJ

SUNDAY JANUARY 5

People and Prayers to Remember this Week

Readings of the Day

Isaiah 60.1-6
Psalm 72

Ephesians 3.2-3a, 5-6
Matthew 2.1-12

Responding to the Word

Isaiah feels like the time of darkness is ended. How has Christ lit up the darkness in my life?

Final Thoughts …

Feasts this Week

January 6	**St André Bessette (USA)**
January 7	**St André Bessette (Canada)**
	St Raymond of Penyafort (USA)
January 8	**St Raymond of Penyafort (Canada)**

SUNDAY JANUARY 12

Baptism of the Lord

BEGINNINGS – WHETHER the first day of school or the first day on a new job, the first day married or as a sister or a priest – not only require us to prepare, but are for us defining moments from which we go forward in some way as a new person. Jesus' baptism is his defining moment. From this moment Jesus lives through three years of preaching and healing, praying, living, dying, and rising. And all of that is rooted in this moment.

Jesus, sharing humanity with us, is drawn to John's baptism of repentance and submits to the cascading water. It is a symbolic act which God transforms into a defining moment: "You are my Son, the Beloved; with you I am well pleased." Words of intense, tender relationship – the core and essence of who Jesus is, what he will do, and why he will do it.

We too have defining moments in our lives. Regardless of whether our eyes see the heavens open or our ears hear a voice, our defining moment is the one where our heart and spirit truly and deeply hear, "YOU are my child. YOU are my Beloved." It is a moment to prepare for, to be ardently thankful for, to live out of the rest of our days. It is the moment we celebrate in the Eucharist.

Sr. Phyllis Giroux, SC

SUNDAY JANUARY 12

People and Prayers to Remember this Week

Readings of the Day

Isaiah 40.1-5, 9-11
Psalm 104

Titus 2.11-14; 3.4-7
Luke 3.15-16, 21-22

Responding to the Word

Isaiah tells us that God is like a shepherd who gathers the lambs in his arms. What part of my life shall I entrust to God's strong arms today?

Final Thoughts ...

Feasts this Week

January 13   **St Hilary**
January 17   **St Anthony**

SUNDAY JANUARY 19
Week of Prayer for Christian Unity

2nd Sunday in Ordinary Time

"Something old, something new; something borrowed, something blue." Many of us remember these old words of advice to brides for their wedding day. Here, at the beginning of the new year, we are conscious of everything being new.

Weddings are new beginnings, aren't they? A couple makes a new beginning together; a new family is started. So it is with the wedding at Cana in today's gospel. The water changing into wine symbolizes the old becoming new. Jesus is showing us that the old order is making way for the new. Bible scholars tell us that with this miracle, Jesus begins his public ministry – this is the beginning of something truly new in the world.

This is Mary's first appearance in John's gospel, and we hear her tell the servants to do whatever her son tells them. Jesus reveals the new order and the disciples believe in him. But what about us? Are we listening to Mary's command to do what her son tells us? Are we like the disciples? Do we truly believe in him? Are we ready to exchange the old order for the new?

If we are ready, we can enter into the new year and new life. We can exchange our old ways, which too often leave us hungering and thirsting. Through Jesus we can enter the new way, if we but believe in him!

Patrick Doyle

SUNDAY JANUARY 19

People and Prayers to Remember this Week

Readings of the Day

Isaiah 62.1-5

1 Corinthians 12.4-11

Psalm 96

John 2.1-12

Responding to the Word

Paul recognizes that each of us has special gifts. What are my gifts and how do I use them?

Final Thoughts …

Feasts this Week

January 20	**St Fabian**
	St Sebastian
January 21	**St Agnes**
January 22	**St Vincent (Canada)**
	Day of Prayer for the Legal Protection of Unborn Children (USA)
January 23	**St Vincent (USA)**
	St Marianne Cope (USA)
January 24	**St Francis de Sales**
January 25	**Conversion of St Paul**

SUNDAY JANUARY 26
Sunday of the Word of God

3rd Sunday in Ordinary Time

We learn from her writings that St Teresa of Avila sat and spoke with Jesus as one would speak with a best friend. One evening, Jesus asked Teresa her name and she replied using her religious name saying, "I am Teresa of Jesus." Teresa was then bold enough to ask Jesus his name, to which Jesus replied, "I am Jesus of Teresa." Teresa – Spanish mystic, Carmelite nun, and renowned author – knew that she and Jesus were one. Today's readings call us to embrace this same truth.

In the first reading, a holy people gather before Ezra to hear the word of God. After listening to the law of the Lord all morning, they shed many tears. They knew they were standing on holy ground. In the second reading, St Paul implores us to recognize that we are holy ground. We are the body of Christ called to do great things.

In the gospel, Jesus recognizes himself as holy ground – called to bring good news to the poor. Can we recognize ourselves as holy ground? In her writings, Teresa of Avila reminds us that Christ has no body now on earth but ours. No hands, no feet on earth but ours. We, the people whom Jesus calls by name, are called to free the oppressed and give sight to the blind. Are we up for the challenge?

Karen Johnson

SUNDAY JANUARY 26

People and Prayers to Remember this Week

Readings of the Day

Nehemiah 8.2-4a, 5-6, 8-10
Psalm 19

1 Corinthians 12.12-30
Luke 1.1-4; 4.14-21

Responding to the Word

Paul knows that we all are joined together into Christ's body. When am I most aware of this Christian unity?

Final Thoughts …

Feasts this Week

January 27	**St Angela Merici**
January 28	**St Thomas Aquinas**
January 31	**St John Bosco**

SUNDAY FEBRUARY 2
World Day for Consecrated Life

The Presentation of the Lord

OUR EXPERIENCE OF the presentation of a baby is always filled with wonder and awe. Now, imagine being present with Simeon and Anna as Mary and Joseph brought Jesus to the temple, in fulfillment of Jewish Law. Simeon and Anna believed, through the prophets, that they would see the Messiah – the redeemer of Jerusalem.

Malachi prophesied that the Lord would come to God's temple. St Paul tells us that we too are God's temples – temples of the Holy Spirit. When Jesus says "Here am I," are we aware, as Simeon and Anna were, of his presence? We readily experience Jesus in the Word, in the Eucharist, and in the sacred; however, we are often blind to his presence in our day-to-day lives.

Our challenge is to become like Anna and Simeon, and to be conscious of Jesus with us: in the quiet and the bustle of our days, in the turmoil and the peace of our world, in the storms and the calm of nature, in the tears and the hopes of our children, in our deepest despair and our every joy.

Let us reflect on the promise of the Advent season, fulfilled in Jesus' birth, witnessed in the Christmas season, and presented to us in every season of our lives.

Susan Berlingeri

SUNDAY FEBRUARY 2

People and Prayers to Remember this Week

Readings of the Day

Malachi 3.1-4　　　　　　　　Hebrews 2.10-11, 13b-18
Psalm 24.　　　　　　　　　　Luke 2.22-40

Responding to the Word

Simeon was able to recognize Jesus as the promised Messiah. Where am I able to recognize Jesus' presence in my life?

Final Thoughts ...

Feasts this Week

February 3	**St Blaise**
	St Ansgar
February 5	**St Agatha**
February 6	**St Paul Miki & Companions**
February 8	**St Jerome Emiliani**
	St Josephine Bakhita

SUNDAY FEBRUARY 9

5th Sunday in Ordinary Time

THE GREATEST MIRACLE of today's gospel reading may not have been that so many fish were caught, filling two boats. Rather, the most astounding miracle could have been that fishermen actually obeyed a carpenter's advice on how and where to do their job!

Many of us are unwilling to listen, much less respond, to the challenge of God's word in our lives. We may feel unworthy. (Could God really be that interested in me?) Certainly we can feel fear at what God's radical message challenges us to do. (Does God really expect me to love my neighbor as myself by visiting the prisoner, clothing the homeless, feeding the hungry?)

Yet here we are asked to consider the example of those who are renowned for giving their entire lives to God: people like Isaiah, Paul, and Simon Peter. Surely they also felt trepidation at hearing God's call, felt themselves unworthy of the challenge put before them and incapable of such faithfulness. Yet, they "put out into the deep" – and it changed their lives forever.

What is it that prevents us from "leaving everything" and following Jesus today? How are we being called, in the everyday events of our own lives? How can God's gift of faith, already present in our hearts, be encouraged to grow and bear fruit in all we do?

Joe Gunn

SUNDAY FEBRUARY 9

People and Prayers to Remember this Week

Readings of the Day

Isaiah 6.1-2a, 3-8
Psalm 138

1 Corinthians 15.1-11
Luke 5.1-11

Responding to the Word

Isaiah learned that God's holy presence makes us more aware of our lack of holiness. From what sinfulness do I want to be cleansed today?

Final Thoughts ...

Feasts this Week

February 10	**St Scholastica**
February 11	**Our Lady of Lourdes**
February 14	**St Cyril & St Methodius**

SUNDAY FEBRUARY 16

6th Sunday in Ordinary Time

CONTRARIES ABOUND IN today's readings. Images of abundance and sterility, blessing and woe, time and eternity engage our imagination. In the first reading, Jeremiah contrasts the blighted state of those who trust in human devices with the blessed state of those who trust in the Lord. For a people with a history of desert wandering, Jeremiah's image of running water, lush greenery, and fruitful abundance would spell blessing indeed.

Jesus' sermon is a vivid example of just how startling the gospel message can be. In fact, it seems to be just the opposite of the "wisdom" pervading our consumer society. Woe, says Jesus, to the rich, the satisfied, the financially secure, and blessing to the poor, the hungry, the suffering. How can this be? Isn't financial security essential to a happy life?

Upon deeper reflection, we see that material acquisition can be isolating. Self-satisfaction, self-absorption are not life-giving but rather leave us uninterested in others. It is when we *lack*, when we have-not, that we are drawn to look beyond ourselves. Our poverty, our hunger, our sorrow can lead to great riches because they invite us into relationship, into community. They call us to deeper friendship with self, God, and others – to compassion, to communion, to love. They open us, in the depth of our humanity, to encounter Christ.

Ella Allen

SUNDAY FEBRUARY 16

People and Prayers to Remember this Week

Readings of the Day

Jeremiah 17.5-8 1 Corinthians 15.12, 16-20
Psalm 1 Luke 6.17, 20-26

Responding to the Word

Jeremiah encourages us to trust in God. What fears make it hard for me to trust?

Final Thoughts ...

Feasts this Week

February 17	**Seven Holy Founders of the Servite Order**
February 21	**St Peter Damian**
February 22	**Chair of St Peter**

SUNDAY FEBRUARY 23

7th Sunday in Ordinary Time

Today's gospel, taken from Luke's version of the Sermon on the Mount, calls us to forgive our enemies. As a person passionate about social justice, I hear this scripture calling me to also consider empathy and dialogue. Can we identify the humanity and the inherent dignity in those who do wrong to us or to others? Can we love them in a way that also works towards addressing these injustices?

To live and love this way can be difficult. It may be easier to see those who hurt ourselves or others as selfish or as intentionally harmful. Yet, that outlook fosters alienation and isolation instead of community and connection. The Gospel recognizes the challenge present here, but encourages us to persist: "If you love those who love you, what credit is that to you? For even sinners love those who love them."

In this gospel, Jesus offers guidance that seems counterintuitive. In the same way, finding common ground with those who oppress others may also be counterintuitive, especially when we are tempted to be angry instead of loving. However, empathy enables us to engage in dialogue, change, and social justice. We can see examples of this in peace processes and efforts towards reconciliation in North America and throughout the world. When we come to a place of understanding, it may also be a place of peace.

Landon Turlock

SUNDAY FEBRUARY 23

People and Prayers to Remember this Week

Readings of the Day

1 Samuel 26.2, 7-9, 12-13, 22-25
Psalm 103

1 Corinthians 15.45-49
Luke 6.27-38

Responding to the Word

Jesus teaches us to love our enemies. Who in my life do I find most difficult to love? Why?

Final Thoughts …

Feasts this Week

February 27   St Gregory of Narek

SUNDAY MARCH 2

8th Sunday in Ordinary Time

I was once on a cave exploration trip in Alberta. Using ropes and special ladders, we went exploring a huge 300-metre-deep cave with a maze of passageways. One guide and I wanted to get to the very bottom. At one point, deep down in the cave, we stopped for a snack. My guide took off his glasses to adjust his helmet. It was complete, utter darkness and dead silence down there. Shortly after leaving our snack spot, my guide noticed he had left his glasses behind. Without his glasses, his eyesight was quite blurred. We never found the glasses. He was no longer able to guide me.

In today's gospel, Jesus says when it comes to really knowing what is in a person's heart, we are like blind guides. We really don't see, even if we think we do. Our eyesight is blocked by our own weaknesses and faults. Jesus invites us to "first take the log out of your own eye." This is about a conversion of heart, grounded in an ongoing prayer life.

The Lord wants to free us of our burdens. We repent, he forgives us, and he helps us change our ways. What joy and freedom! Thus, with the psalmist, we want to declare his "steadfast love in the morning," and his "faithfulness by night."

Emmanuel Martel

SUNDAY MARCH 2

People and Prayers to Remember this Week

Readings of the Day

Sirach 27.4-7
Psalm 92

1 Corinthians 15.54-58
Luke 6.39-45

Responding to the Word

Jesus teaches us not to judge others. Who in my life do I most often want to correct? Why?

Final Thoughts ...

Feasts this Week

March 3	**St Katharine Drexel (USA)**
March 4	**St Casimir**
March 5	**Ash Wednesday**
March 7	**St Perpetua & St Felicity**
March 8	**St John of God**

WEDNESDAY MARCH 5

Ash Wednesday

Today, as we begin the season of Lent, the gospel reading gives us some tips on the *do's* and *don'ts* of our traditional Lenten practices.

In the gospel, Jesus contrasts the proud behavior of the hypocrites with the attitude of humility that characterizes a true disciple. The hypocrites love to make a show of their spiritual practices; in contrast, Jesus instructs his disciples to do good quietly, to pray privately, and to fast with a sense of dignified joy.

The hypocrites' showy displays of piety neither please nor fool God. There is a similar message in the reading from the prophet Joel. The contrite heart pleases God more than the outward signs of fasting: "rend your hearts and not your clothing," says the Lord.

When our hearts are properly disposed, our Lenten observances help us to refocus our attention on God, to restore our relationship with God, and to recommit our lives to God. Prayer opens our hearts and minds to God. Acts of self-denial help us to detach from the things that distract us from God. Acts of charity express our participation with Jesus in proclaiming the kingdom of God.

During our celebration of the liturgy today, let us receive the ashes with joy, ever mindful, as St Paul writes to the Corinthians, that the time of salvation is now!

Louise McEwan

WEDNESDAY MARCH 5

People and Prayers to Remember this Week

Readings of the Day

Joel 2.12-18
Psalm 51

2 Corinthians 5.20 – 6.2
Matthew 6.1-6, 16-18

Responding to the Word

Jesus teaches that prayer, almsgiving, and fasting should be done in secret. What good deeds can I do in secret during this Lent?

Final Thoughts …

SUNDAY MARCH 9

1st Sunday of Lent

When we were re-landscaping our yard a few years ago, we decided to get rid of a juniper tree, thinking it would be a simple process. Wrong! We dug, we chopped, we pulled. Nothing! It was so firmly rooted that we ended up pulling it out with a truck.

I think of that juniper today when reflecting on Jesus' temptations in the desert. No matter what the devil said or offered, Jesus remained firmly rooted in God's word. The lure of comfort and wealth and power was no match for what Jesus knew to be ultimately true as revealed in Scripture.

Many people view Lent negatively – as a time of deprivation and denial. Today's gospel reminds us instead that Lent is a time to become more solidly grounded in our faith. Making more time for prayer and Scripture, fasting from things in our lives that keep us from giving ourselves wholeheartedly to God, giving of ourselves in service to others: far from depriving us, these are the tools we can use to ensure that we are firmly rooted in the things of God.

As we continue our Lenten journey, may we be strengthened to follow in the footsteps of the One who unflinchingly stood up to evil and ultimately triumphed over it.

Teresa Whalen Lux

SUNDAY MARCH 9

People and Prayers to Remember this Week

Readings of the Day

Deuteronomy 26.4-10
Psalm 91

Romans 10.8-13
Luke 4.1-13

Responding to the Word

God is near us through God's own word in Scripture and in our hearts. What do I need to do to be more attentive to how God might want to communicate with me today?

Final Thoughts ...

SUNDAY MARCH 16

2nd Sunday of Lent

TODAY'S GOSPEL STORY is astounding! Jesus took three disciples with him to a mountaintop to pray. Before their very eyes, his appearance was gloriously transformed. Two prophets from long ago then appeared and spoke with Jesus about his imminent death. Can we even *begin* to imagine the emotions that surface in the three as they witness the unfolding scene? No strangers to Jesus' miracles, even they must have agreed that this moment surpassed anything that they had ever seen!

Although filled with a desire to sleep, "they stayed awake" and beheld the ultimate splendor of Jesus. They heard the voice of his father proclaim, "This is my Son, my Chosen; listen to him!" What was their inner response? Fear? Awe and wonder? A deepened awareness of the identity of Jesus? A new sense of mission?

As followers of Jesus, we, too, must "stay awake" to recognize his presence in the myriad situations of our lives. We don't hear God's voice coming from a cloud, but when we listen, we hear his voice in the silence of our hearts. God also speaks to us through contemporary prophets who guide us on our spiritual journey.

At the moment of the Transfiguration, Peter and his companions beheld the face of Jesus. Our hearts longingly cry out, "Your face, O Lord, do I seek."

Barbara d'Artois

SUNDAY MARCH 16

People and Prayers to Remember this Week

Readings of the Day

Genesis 15.5-12, 17-18
Psalm 27

Philippians 3.17 – 4.1
Luke 9.28b-36

Responding to the Word

Paul knows we are being transformed as Christ was. What new life from Christ is transforming me this Lent?

Final Thoughts ...

Feasts this Week

March 17	St Patrick
March 18	St Cyril of Jerusalem
March 19	St Joseph

SUNDAY MARCH 23

3rd Sunday of Lent

"May your life be fruitful." Years ago, these words were solemnly and sincerely spoken to me. In our own way, each of us receives this same blessing. During Lent, we are invited to reflect on the fruitfulness of our lives. Every one of us is created to do more than take up space in the garden.

Jesus, in telling the parable of the barren fig tree, teaches us something important. As gardener, he takes an active role in our lives, promising to rework and renew the soil. Gardeners know these unglamorous tasks are essential for producing abundant fruit.

Jesus lovingly commits himself to the troubles and trials of our lives. The wise gardener, he knows when and how to amend the soil. Tended carefully, even the least appealing aspects of our lives offer essential nutrients for healthy growth. We can be transformed; our lives can become ever more fruitful.

Our "yes" to this growth lies in our personal willingness to repent. Twice in this gospel, Jesus emphasizes his lack of concern over who is a worse sinner or a worse offender. He simply looks for our willingness to be renewed.

At every Eucharist, we renew our "yes." We pray, acknowledging our need for our Lord: "only say the word and my soul shall be healed." May our lives be fruitful.

Brenda Merk Hildebrand

SUNDAY MARCH 23

People and Prayers to Remember this Week

Readings of the Day

Exodus 3.1-8a, 13-15
Psalm 103

1 Corinthians 10.1-6, 10-12
Luke 13.1-9

Responding to the Word

Moses learns that where God is present is holy ground. Where have I most experienced God's presence creating a holy place or situation?

Final Thoughts ...

Feasts this Week

March 25 Annunciation of the Lord

SUNDAY MARCH 30

4th Sunday of Lent

THE YOUNGER SON in today's parable experienced twists and turns on life's journey, before he "came to himself." We all need to "come to ourselves" – to know who we really are. Our good and loving God created us to be people of love and goodness. We've been given gifts and talents, for our good and the good of others. We've been created with great dignity and great responsibility.

Often, we forget that. We get lost, go astray: we make the wrong choices, take the wrong path. We need to "come to ourselves" – to remember who we are. Scripture, prayer, reconciliation, Eucharist: they help us to find our way.

Maybe our getting lost or forgetting who we are is not as extreme as with the younger son, but it still happens. It happened to the older son. He, too, needed to come to himself. His father had to remind him: "Son, you are always with me, and all that is mine is yours." We need to hear that, too. We need to know that God created us in love and calls us into relationship. When we lose track of that, we don't live as we should: we aren't being the people God meant us to be. We all need to be reminded of who we really are, so we can live from that fullness.

Dinah Simmons

SUNDAY MARCH 30

People and Prayers to Remember this Week

Readings of the Day

Joshua 5.9a, 10-12
Psalm 34

2 Corinthians 5.17-21
Luke 15.1-3, 11-32

Responding to the Word

As Christians we are reconciled with God and become ministers of reconciliation. How might I be a minister of reconciliation this week?

Final Thoughts …

Feasts this Week

April 2 St Francis of Paola
April 4 St Isidore
April 5 St Vincent Ferrer

SUNDAY APRIL 6

5th Sunday of Lent

Leaving old ways behind is not easy. Today's readings remind us that breaking away from the past is essential to obtaining eternal life with Jesus Christ.

After the Pharisees and scribes accuse a woman of committing adultery, Jesus provides them with the opportunity to examine their own consciences and move to a new life centered on forgiveness. They choose to walk away, silently rejecting this invitation.

It is the woman who gains freedom from her past. With her accusers gone, she is no longer bound by their punishment. But her true freedom comes from the forgiveness Jesus gives her. She is left alone with this man who gives her a new chance at life. Her only instruction is to go on her way and not sin again.

Never sinning again is impossible, as we often repeat past mistakes. However, the Lord's mercy is infinite and if we continue to seek forgiveness for our sins, he grants it. In this way we can work on our transgressions, leaving them behind and entering into a Christ-centered life. This work is hard, but by keeping our hearts open, we can receive Jesus' forgiveness as well as strength to begin anew.

Elizabeth Chesley-Jewell

SUNDAY APRIL 6

People and Prayers to Remember this Week

Readings of the Day

Isaiah 43.16-21
Psalm 126

Philippians 3.8-14
John 8.1-11

Responding to the Word

Paul's losses seem small when compared with his gain of having Christ in his life. What have I already gained by seeking Christ this Lent?

Final Thoughts …

Feasts this Week

April 7   **St John Baptist de la Salle**
April 11   **St Stanislaus**

SUNDAY APRIL 13

Passion (Palm) Sunday

EVERY YEAR, THE Church in her wisdom gives us a window into Christ's suffering, so that we might understand the love that compelled him. "Jesus took his place at the table, and the Apostles with him." I was struck that these are words that begin the telling of the Passion of Christ in Luke's gospel. Jesus is taking his place, in place of us.

He took his place as the sacrificial lamb during the Passover meal. Then, he took his place in humble service. He took his place in cautioning against doubt, fear – but mostly despair. He took his place being counted among the wicked, losing all his social standing. He took his place interceding for us, then, in undergoing scurrilous insults. He took his place in being convicted while innocent, while watching an ungrateful, guilty criminal walk free.

As the painful description of our Lord's suffering continues, we see something else unfold. He received. He received help, care, even pity. He received the final punishment with its nails and the crown of thorns. While he received the judgment of the world upon himself, he received the repentant sinner, hung alongside him. This is how our Savior lived. And died.

When you receive Our Lord in the Eucharist, do so gratefully, humbly, and confidently. For God so loved the world that he gave all. For you.

Johanne Brownrigg

SUNDAY APRIL 13

People and Prayers to Remember this Week

Readings of the Day

Luke 19.28-40 (Procession)
Isaiah 50.4-7
Psalm 22

Philippians 2.6-11
Luke 22.14 – 23.56

Responding to the Word

God's servant desires to speak an encouraging word to the weary. Who needs to hear a good word from me today?

Final Thoughts …

THURSDAY APRIL 17
Mass of the Lord's Supper

Holy Thursday

Although Peter, in his culture, would have been familiar with foot-washing as a practical act of hospitality towards weary travelers, he was initially uncomfortable allowing Jesus to do this for him. Had we attended the Last Supper ourselves, we might also have protested, out of a real sense of the incongruity of a master washing a disciple's feet.

Post-resurrection, though, and with the aid of the Spirit, we disciples now understand the many dimensions of this profound sign. We recognize in Jesus' humble action towards "his own" yet another example of his self-sacrificial love, laying down both his outer garb and his very life for our sake. We are reminded, too, of the many ways in which we share in Christ's paschal mystery: through the entire sacramental life of the Church, and in the myriad other ways in which the ordained and common priesthoods share in Christ's priestly, prophetic, and royal offices. We acknowledge with gratitude an act of hospitality on Jesus' part, welcoming us into his eternal home.

Still, becoming comfortable with, and accepting, the unfailing Divine Love at the core of the relationship between God and human beings is a lifelong effort. Renewing our "share" with Jesus, may our Triduum celebrations free us to love others as Jesus has loved us.

Christine Mader

THURSDAY APRIL 17

People and Prayers to Remember Today

Readings of the Day

Exodus 12.1-8, 11-14
Psalm 116

1 Corinthians 11.23-26
John 13.1-15

Responding to the Word

God tells the Israelites to make their family meal holy. How might I make my household meals more holy?

Final Thoughts ...

FRIDAY APRIL 18
Celebration of the Lord's Passion

Good Friday

TODAY'S GOSPEL IS fundamental in many ways. The entire history of the world, from the moment Adam and Eve ate the apple, has led to this moment. From the Great Flood, to the Exodus, to the Ten Commandments, to the kings and prophets of old – all is in preparation for this moment.

For today, God fulfills his promise from long ago. When Adam and Eve sinned, an immeasurable separation was made between humanity and God, one that we could never fix. However, God never abandons his children. Jesus shows himself for who he truly is and why he came to the earth. Jesus is so much more than a prophet, a king, a teacher, a healer, an exorcist, or a miracle-worker. He is God, our Savior.

The day our first parents fell, God promised to save us. In his suffering and death on the cross, Jesus fulfills this promise and restores our relationship with God. This is the purpose of his life. Jesus is the bridge between heaven and earth. If you haven't crossed it, God invites you to do so now. All you have to do is have faith in Jesus Christ and repent of your sins. There is no better time to give your life to Jesus. May you do so now.

Connor Brownrigg

FRIDAY APRIL 18

People and Prayers to Remember Today

Readings of the Day

Isaiah 52.13 – 53.12
Psalm 31

Hebrews 4.14-16; 5.7-9
John 18.1 – 19.42

Responding to the Word

Jesus sympathizes with our weakness. What weakness do I want to acknowledge to Jesus today?

Final Thoughts …

SATURDAY APRIL 19
Resurrection of the Lord

Easter Vigil

It is easy to think that if we had been present for God's great saving acts, detailed in the readings of the Easter Vigil and culminating in the Resurrection, then faith would be easy. If only we had seen, then we would believe. But St Paul says faith comes from hearing (Rom 10.17). Our resurrection story from Luke supports this idea. Even the first witnesses to the resurrection struggled to understand what their eyes told them. An empty tomb is not, automatically, good news. The women only understood and believed after the angels gave the explanation: "He is not here, but has risen."

The women, in turn, tell the disciples. The women had seen, but needed hearing to understand. Now these men have heard, but need to see. Only one even took the time to look. But when Peter did, he found it just as the women had said.

God is active in our lives even today. But we often fail to recognize such action for what it is. Faith, which God gives us through the community of faith, the Church, where we hear the story, gives us the lens to see what God is doing. If we take the time to look into what we have heard, we might see something that leaves us as amazed as Peter.

Brett Salkeld

SATURDAY APRIL 19

People and Prayers to Remember Today

Readings of the Day

Genesis 1.1 – 2.2
Psalm 104 or Psalm 33
Genesis 22.1-18
Psalm 16
Exodus 14.15-31; 15.20, 1
Exodus 15
Isaiah 54.5-14
Psalm 30
Isaiah 55.1-11

Isaiah 12
Baruch 3.9-15, 32 – 4.4
Psalm 19
Ezekiel 36.16-17a, 18-28
Psalm 42 or Psalm 51
Romans 6.3-11
Psalm 118
Luke 24.1-12

Responding to the Word

Paul reminds us that our union with Jesus will bring us to new life. What new life has begun in me during this Lent?

Final Thoughts …

SUNDAY APRIL 20
Resurrection of the Lord

Easter Sunday

A DARK MORNING – it seems like the world is ending. There is nothing left, no future, only sadness... even the tomb is empty. No comfort to be found in grieving. If only time could turn back!

Mary stands, weeping, outside the darkened tomb. She is bereft, hoping against hope, but now she is unable even to gaze on the lifeless body of her beloved Jesus.

Unless we have suffered the loss of someone close to us, it is impossible to understand death. But this is even worse – a disappearance, obliteration.

Then suddenly, Jesus appears and the darkness engulfing her soul is lifted. We can imagine it is as if light is bursting forth from the tomb. It sounds like a fairy tale, but this is no fairy tale.

This is Easter, the Resurrection. A new world was born that morning when Jesus stepped out of the tomb where he had lain for three days. The sin which brought darkness was obliterated and the world began anew, bathed in the light of the resurrection.

This miracle isn't confined to that historical event some 2,000 years ago. It is alive this Easter morning, and it is alive every Sunday morning when we re-create the life, death, and resurrection of Jesus.

This is the miracle: the light of Christ banishes the darkness of hopelessness.

Patrick M. Doyle

SUNDAY APRIL 20

People and Prayers to Remember this Week

Readings of the Day

Acts 10.34a, 37-43
Psalm 118
Colossians 3.1-4
or 1 Corinthians 5.6b-8

John 20.1-18
or Luke 24.1-12
or Luke 24.13-35

Responding to the Word

Paul encourages us to live in a new way because of our relationship with Christ. What new behaviors will I adopt to be more like Jesus?

Final Thoughts …

SUNDAY APRIL 27
Divine Mercy Sunday

2nd Sunday of Easter

When there is a crisis or a tragedy, we eagerly await the first words of those who've come through the trauma. Knowing their survival is exceptional, we hang on their every word. They are charged with so much meaning!

With this kind of anticipation, we ask today: What were some of Jesus' first words as he emerged from his tomb? "Peace be with you," he announced – a message repeated again and again in the gospels. What is this "peace" – a word that is time-worn in our day – that carries such an extraordinary meaning in today's gospel?

John's gospel tells of a deep personal peace that comes when we are freed from fear and confusion. Jesus indicates this freedom as he asks doubting Thomas to feel his wounds, dissolving Thomas' fear and distrust by letting himself be touched so intimately.

Here we witness a major point in today's story: Jesus does not merely suggest we come to peace; he takes us by the hand and initiates the way for us to do so. A friend doesn't merely cajole a fearful friend; they reach out and touch that person – in a real and peace-filled way.

Jesus shows us the way, providing us with not only first words but also first actions – after emerging from the tomb. In this way, he instructs us to go and do the same.

Jerome Herauf

SUNDAY APRIL 27

People and Prayers to Remember this Week

Readings of the Day

Acts 5.12-16
Psalm 118

Revelation 1.9-11a, 12-13, 17-19
John 20.19-31

Responding to the Word

The risen Jesus tells John not to be afraid. What fears about Christ's presence to me must I overcome?

Final Thoughts …

Feasts this Week

April 28	**St Peter Chanel**
	St Louis Grignion de Montfort
April 29	**St Catherine of Siena**
April 30	**St Marie of the Incarnation (Canada)**
	St Pius V (USA)
May 1	**St Joseph the Worker**
	St Pius V (Canada)
May 2	**St Athanasius**
May 3	**St Philip & St James**

SUNDAY MAY 4

3rd Sunday of Easter

God lovingly pursues us, calling us far beyond our own safety zones to share the good news of salvation. We see this clearly in the life of the apostle Peter.

He was chosen for discipleship by Jesus but he had a hard time. When Jesus was brought before the high priest, Peter was so afraid that he denied three times that he was Christ's disciple. After he saw Jesus' empty tomb, he went home and locked all the doors. When it looked like the great adventure with Jesus was a miserable failure, he went back to what he knew: his fishing boat.

However, the promise of Easter was genuine. Jesus really did rise from the dead. He met Simon Peter on his own territory, when he was fishing, and called him again. Call and response were unmistakable. Three times, Jesus asks "Do you love me?" Peter's answers were "Yes," "Yes," and "Yes I do, and I already told you I did."

Jesus tells Peter to take care of the flock, prepare for difficult times, and "follow me." Peter did that. So today, all around the world, we are still responding to God's call, still daring to take risks in service to the proclamation of God's unending love. We are compelled to share the good news of Jesus Christ, risen from the dead. Alleluia!

Marilyn J. Sweet

SUNDAY MAY 4

People and Prayers to Remember this Week

Readings of the Day

Acts 5.27-32, 40b-41
Psalm 30

Revelation 5.11-14
John 21.1-19

Responding to the Word

When Peter recognizes Jesus, nothing can hold him back. What might be holding me back from being with Jesus?

Final Thoughts ...

Feasts this Week

May 6 St François de Laval (Canada)
May 8 Bl Catherine of St Augustine (Canada)
May 10 St John of Avila
           St Damien de Veuster (USA)

SUNDAY MAY 11
World Day of Prayer for Vocations

4th Sunday of Easter

Once, when out hiking in the forest, my wife and I lost track of our little girl. Holding our son close and shouting out our daughter's name, we spent anxious moments frantically searching for her in the bush. Only a parent can know the relief we felt upon discovering her to be safe and sound.

Or, perhaps, could a shepherd also be familiar with such emotion?

Jesus, the Good Shepherd, says "My sheep know my voice." This suggests that the first step on the road to follow Jesus is to listen. To have familiarity, even intimacy, with the voice of the Good Shepherd means to spend time listening to the Word of God.

But Jesus' teaching on the Good Shepherd suggests more is then required of us: "I know them, and they follow me." After listening, we must respond to the embrace of the Good Shepherd. Discerning our own specific vocation, we ask how this journey can take us yet closer to God.

Paul's and Barnabas' vocation was to preach the Word, even when opposed. Jesus found his own message contested and contradicted by the religious authorities; they even wanted to stone him. While it is unlikely this would happen to us today, it is always good to ask: how I can respond to the loving call of the Good Shepherd through my actions this week?

Joe Gunn

SUNDAY MAY 11

People and Prayers to Remember this Week

Readings of the Day

Acts 13.14, 43-52
Psalm 100

Revelation 7.9, 14b-17
John 10.27-30

Responding to the Word

Despite problems, the disciples were filled with joy. What joy have I felt during this Easter season?

Final Thoughts ...

Feasts this Week

May 12	**St Nereus & St Achilleus**
	St Pancras
May 13	**Our Lady of Fatima**
May 14	**St Matthias**
May 15	**St Isidore (USA)**

SUNDAY MAY 18

5th Sunday of Easter

Today we read, "When Judas had gone out, Jesus said, 'Now the Son of Man has been glorified, and God has been glorified in him.'" This is Jesus' surprising response to betrayal by a good friend! How can this moment of disloyalty be a moment of glory?

To glorify someone is to recognize them as God knows them and announce it to the world. On special birthdays in my family, we make up a list of things that are true about someone and read them at the party. We might say, "You are a good artist, cook, or teacher" or "You are gentle, patient, or a good listener." People respond with a mixture of embarrassment and delight. Sometimes the statement recognizes a painful truth. "You suffered through your illness gracefully and that gave me strength to face my struggles. Thank you!" These are particularly awkward and beautiful moments. We are distinguishing someone for their capacity to live suffering in a way that gives life to others. We are naming grace and expressing our gratitude for how it touched our lives. We are praising God in this moment because we know that grace is God working in our life.

Jesus and God are glorified by Judas' betrayal because Jesus does not retaliate but lives his suffering with gentleness and strength, and that gives life to us.

Joseph Vorstermans

SUNDAY MAY 18

People and Prayers to Remember this Week

Readings of the Day

Acts 14.21-27
Psalm 145

Revelation 21.1-5a
John 13.1, 31-33a, 34-35

Responding to the Word

Jesus declares that his followers will be known by their love. Who have been encouraging examples for me of the kind of self-sacrificing love that Jesus showed?

Final Thoughts …

Feasts this Week

May 20	**St Bernardine of Siena**
May 21	**St Eugène de Mazenod (Canada)**
	St Christopher Magallanes & Companions
May 22	**St Rita of Cascia**
May 24	**Bl Louis-Zépherin Moreau (Canada)**

SUNDAY MAY 25

6th Sunday of Easter

On the night before he dies, Jesus is with his disciples. Having washed their feet in an act of humble service as an example to them, he proceeds to share with them his last hopes and dreams and promises. His ministry on this earth is nearing its end; yet, in another way, it is only beginning.

We are there, listening to these last words, because they are for us, too. We, too, carry on Jesus' mission. The promise given to the disciples – and to us – is peace. Peace is Jesus' farewell to us, his gift to us. What more can he give? What more do we need? It is not the kind of peace we might expect. It is not an easy peace. His gift of peace is wrapped in the challenge of loving service, compassionate inclusion, and courageous integrity. Accepting the gift means to live as Jesus lived.

Following the path laid out for us by Jesus is possible when we are immersed in a eucharistic community. When we come together to celebrate the life, death, and resurrection of the Lord, we become what we receive. Our life takes on a new dimension and we experience the depth of God's presence in us and among us. God's promise is fulfilled.

Sr. Mary Ellen Green, OP

SUNDAY MAY 25

People and Prayers to Remember this Week

Readings of the Day

Acts 15.1-2, 22-29
Psalm 67

Revelation 21.10-14, 22-23
John 14.23-29

Responding to the Word

Though he will no longer be visible, Jesus promises to be with us in Spirit. When have I felt Jesus' presence with me recently?

Final Thoughts ...

Feasts this Week

May 26	**St Philip Neri**
May 27	**St Augustine of Canterbury**
May 29	**St Paul VI**
	Ascension of the Lord (in some dioceses of the USA)
May 31	**Visitation of the Blessed Virgin Mary**

SUNDAY JUNE 1
World Communications Day

Ascension of the Lord*

LIFE, IT SEEMS, is full of goodbyes. Children leave the nest, family and friends move away, or a loved one dies. Sometimes we feel only a gentle sadness tempered by hope; other times our hearts are broken by grief.

In today's gospel, the disciples are once again saying goodbye to Jesus. As he prepares to depart from this earth, he offers them some parting gifts: the gift of understanding, so that they can now fully comprehend the meaning of the Scriptures; the promise that they will receive the power of the Holy Spirit; a final loving blessing.

The reaction of the disciples shows a striking transformation. Luke tells us that they returned to Jerusalem with great joy, praising and worshiping God. How different this is from the frightened little band who had cowered indoors after the crucifixion. Now they are clearly filled with the Holy Spirit. Their eyes and hearts are opened, and their faith and courage are strong as they undertake their mission to be witnesses and proclaimers of the Good News.

May we, his disciples today, recognize and celebrate the ongoing presence of Jesus in our lives, and the power of the Spirit to transform and heal even our deepest fears.

Krystyna Higgins

*The 7th Sunday of Easter is celebrated in some dioceses of the USA today. Refer to p. 108.

SUNDAY JUNE 1

People and Prayers to Remember this Week

Readings of the Day

Acts 1.1-11
Psalm 47
Ephesians 1.17-23

or Hebrews 9.24-28; 10.19-23
Luke 24.46-53

Responding to the Word

Although Jesus departs, he promises empowerment by the Holy Spirit for the apostles' ministry. When have I felt most empowered by the Holy Spirit?

Final Thoughts ...

Feasts this Week

June 2	**St Marcellinus & St Peter**
June 3	**St Charles Lwanga & Companions**
June 5	**St Boniface**
June 6	**St Norbert**

SUNDAY JUNE 1
World Communications Day

7th Sunday of Easter (USA)

FOR MANY CHRISTIANS, religious formation included learning why our teachings are right and those of other Christian churches are wrong. This was not merely an intellectual exercise. The "others" were frequently rejected, labeled heretics and shunned. Thousands, if not millions, of people were killed because we built walls instead of bridges.

One reasonable conclusion from today's gospel is that Jesus does not like walls and exclusion. In his lengthy prayer at the Last Supper, Jesus asks the Father that his disciples "may be one, as we are one, I in them and you in me." This is an astounding notion – that God's people, through Jesus, may share in the life of the Trinity. If we are Christians, it is thus impossible for us to be divided.

Jesus says nothing about dogmatic agreement. He simply prays that all may be one "so that the world may believe you have sent me." Nothing is more basic to being Christian than being in union with Jesus and other Christians. It is also crucial to spreading the faith.

If we want to know why the Western world is turning away from Christ, we could look at ourselves. The lack of Christian unity is a scandal that prevents people from accepting the faith. Why do we refuse to carry out Christ's will?

Glen Argan

SUNDAY JUNE 1

People and Prayers to Remember this Week

Readings of the Day

Acts 7.55-60
Psalm 97

Revelation 22.12-14, 16-17, 20
John 17.20-26

Responding to the Word

Stephen was stoned for his faith in Jesus Christ. When did I have to witness to my faith in Jesus at great personal cost?

Final Thoughts ...

SUNDAY JUNE 8

Pentecost Sunday

THE RISEN CHRIST is not deterred by locked doors – or locked hearts.

The apostles were locked behind closed doors, literally and figuratively. They were locked in the upper room, fearful of the authorities. They were also locked inside their own fear, anger, guilt, and grief... and Jesus broke through all of that.

He appeared suddenly in their midst and shared with them the first gifts of the resurrection: forgiveness and peace. He commissioned them to share those gifts with others. He sent them out, as the Father had sent him.

The peace of the Risen Lord, and all the gifts of his Spirit, would unlock the door of the upper room... and also unlock the disciples' hearts and lives. We see this in Acts, where the peace and joy they have received are communicated to others: Jews and non-Jews, strangers from many countries, people of many languages. The gifts the apostles received were sharable – more than that, contagious – and they were available for everyone. Not just a select few. Everyone.

A universal language was spoken by the apostles on Pentecost: the language of love, peace, forgiveness, hope... the story of God's mighty deeds... the call to discipleship, to a life of love and self-giving. This call could be heard and understood by everyone: a call into relationship, with Christ and with one another.

Dinah Simmons

SUNDAY JUNE 8

People and Prayers to Remember this Week

Readings of the Day

Acts 2.1-11
Psalm 104
1 Corinthians 12.3b-7, 12-13

or Romans 8.8-17
John 20.19-23
or John 14.15-16, 23b-26

Responding to the Word

We have all been gifted by the Holy Spirit. What spiritual gifts have I been given and how am I using them?

Final Thoughts …

Feasts this Week

June 9 Blessed Virgin Mary, Mother of the Church
June 11 St Barnabas
June 13 St Anthony of Padua

SUNDAY JUNE 15

Most Holy Trinity

WHILE THE MYSTERY of God is beyond our comprehension, today's readings offer a tangible connection to God's great wisdom. We begin with a front-row seat at the creation of the universe: God, with Wisdom at his side, delighting in the work of all creation. With humble awe, we receive glory and honor beyond our understanding.

On one level, we know many things. We know we are created in the image and likeness of God, the Creator. We know God's very being walked on this earth, in the person of his son, Jesus Christ. We know that when Jesus returned home to the Father, he sent his Spirit to teach and guide us.

On another level, we cannot comprehend the "why" of it all. Wisely, we turn to a question we can answer: "How?" Whenever we delight in creation, we are in harmony with our Creator. We honor the Redeemer by living with faith, hope, and love. Quietly attentive, we hear in our hearts the whispered wisdom of the Sanctifier.

Each time we bless ourselves with the Sign of the Cross, we are acknowledging the mystery of the threefold presence. Refreshing ourselves in Word and Sacrament, we receive the grace to live holy and sacred lives. Rejoicing, we share in God's sense of delight.

Brenda Merk Hildebrand

SUNDAY JUNE 15

People and Prayers to Remember this Week

Readings of the Day

Proverbs 8.22-31
Psalm 8

Romans 5.1-5
John 16.12-15

Responding to the Word

The Holy Spirit will guide us to all truth. With what difficulties do I most need the Spirit's guidance today?

Final Thoughts …

Feasts this Week

June 19   **St Romuald**
June 21   **St Aloysius Gonzaga**

SUNDAY JUNE 22

Body and Blood of Christ

TODAY WE JOIN the crowds following Jesus. Our hearts are afire with anticipation and joy as he speaks about the kingdom of God. To hear his voice, to walk in his presence, to see him healing the sick with gentleness and compassion touches our hearts with wonder.

Jesus receives the people and speaks to them about the kingdom of God, and he heals those who need to be cured. Above all, he feeds them, the five thousand, "with five loaves and two fish" and when the leftovers are gathered up, they fill twelve baskets. This miracle foreshadows God's great love for us and his abundance through the Eucharist.

Come to the feast with trust and hope and belief that God will always provide, and that God is present in the celebration of the Eucharist. It is here that we are fed with the body and blood of Christ and are satisfied. It is here that we come for forgiveness and it is here that we are nourished by God's everlasting love.

Today's readings center on God's presence and intervention in the lives of people down through the ages. God continues to be with us today in and through the gift of the Eucharist. Our response is one of praise and thanksgiving to Almighty God for the gift of everlasting love, freely given to us.

Sr. Johanna d'Agostino, IBVM

SUNDAY JUNE 22

People and Prayers to Remember this Week

Readings of the Day

Genesis 14.18-20
Psalm 110

1 Corinthians 11.23-26
Luke 9.11b-17

Responding to the Word

The wondrous sharing of Jesus' bread is continued in our Eucharist. How might I, like Jesus, share my bread and myself more with others?

Final Thoughts …

Feasts this Week

June 24	**Nativity of St John the Baptist**
June 27	**Most Sacred Heart of Jesus**
June 28	**St Irenaeus**
	Immaculate Heart of Mary

SUNDAY JUNE 29

St Peter and St Paul

It is easy to lose the point in familiar passages. Today's gospel is one of those. We often focus on Peter's confession and its relationship to the Church and forget the beginning. Did you notice it? Jesus asked the disciples "But who do you say that I am?" He is asking for a decision, a verdict, or perhaps even, as Peter offers, a confession of faith. The issue is not who others say Jesus is – what they think about him – but who they personally think he is.

It is not enough to know about Jesus. The people of ancient Israel knew a lot about Jesus: Jesus is John the Baptist returned from the dead; a great prophet like the prophets of old; maybe even the militant Messiah come to free the country from the Romans and set up a new kingdom of Israel.

What is needed is not to *know about* Jesus but to *know* Jesus. The former is facts, knowledge. The latter is a personal relationship.

We might reword Jesus' question to read "You – what do you think of me?" Our knowledge of Jesus must never be second-hand. It must come from personal discovery. We might think we know all there is to know about Jesus and yet still not know Jesus. Jesus is demanding of us – and not simply of the disciples – a personal verdict: "You – what do you think?"

Rev. James B. Sauer

SUNDAY JUNE 29

People and Prayers to Remember this Week

Readings of the Day

Acts 12.1-11
Psalm 34

2 Timothy 4.6-8, 17-18
Matthew 16.13-19

Responding to the Word

Peter declares Jesus to be the Messiah. Who is Jesus for me in my life?

Final Thoughts …

Feasts this Week

June 30	**First Martyrs of the Holy Roman Church**
July 1	**St Junípero Serra (USA)**
	Canada Day (Canada)
July 3	**St Thomas**
July 4	**St Elizabeth of Portugal (Canada)**
	Independence Day (USA)
July 5	**St Anthony Zaccaria**
	St Elizabeth of Portugal (USA)

SUNDAY JULY 6

14th Sunday in Ordinary Time

THE GOSPEL TODAY repeats the phrase, "the kingdom of God has come near." This repetition in the reading emphasizes that God's kingdom is at the heart of the proclamation of the gospel. These early followers of Christ are sent out to share the fact that God is close at hand. God's very love and mercy are made present in their works as the sick are healed, evil is banished, and peace is manifest. Even in those places where the message is rejected, Jesus tells his followers to say that God's kingdom is near.

In other words, the kingdom of God is not something that ultimately can be rejected. Jesus assures his followers that they have been given power over wolves, snakes, and scorpions and he promises that nothing will harm them. God's healing love, mercy, and justice always prevail, even over what appears to be rejection of this powerful, life-changing message.

We, today's followers of Christ, are sent out in the same way to spread the good news of God's healing presence and forgiving love. We, too, are called to remember that even though God's word is not always heard or accepted, the experience of God's kingdom prevails. The Eucharist is our constant reminder of this enduring love and saving power. The kingdom of God is indeed near; let us rejoice and give thanks.

Beth McIsaac Bruce

SUNDAY JULY 6

People and Prayers to Remember this Week

Readings of the Day

Isaiah 66.10-14
Psalm 66

Galatians 6.14-18
Luke 10.1-12, 17-20

Responding to the Word

Old status markers like circumcision mean nothing to Paul because of his relation to Christ. How has my faith made me rethink worldly honors?

Final Thoughts …

Feasts this Week

July 9   **St Augustine Zhao Rong & Companions**
July 11   **St Benedict**

SUNDAY JULY 13

15th Sunday in Ordinary Time

"Do this, and you will live." Doesn't everyone want to know the secret to eternal life? But when I read that I must love God and my neighbor, my enthusiasm dissipates. I've heard it before. I was hoping for something more.

It's as if Jesus anticipates my response, and he doesn't let me down. In the parable of the Good Samaritan, Jesus goes on to provide the example of mercy lived well. Jesus challenges us to put our time, talent, and treasure at the service of our neighbor. To reach out to the homeless stranger on a downtown street, the hurting teenager next door, and the elderly relative who yearns for a visitor – or even a phone call. My spirit sags: O Lord, too often I have failed to love and show mercy.

I can sense God looking at me, still patient but a little weary, wondering why so many reminders are necessary. Before I can get too worked up over my failings, Jesus delivers the proverbial kick in the seat of the pants, saying, "Go and do likewise."

Jesus knows we remain works in progress and so he persists. He calls us to imitate him, to dig deeper, to love and show mercy to all, every day, with no time-outs. We are wise when we heed Jesus' example and his words: "Do this, and you will live."

Harry McAvoy

SUNDAY JULY 13

People and Prayers to Remember this Week

Readings of the Day

Deuteronomy 30.10-14
Psalm 69 or Psalm 19

Colossians 1.15-20
Luke 10.25-37

Responding to the Word

Jesus praises the one who overcame his prejudices and acted out of compassion. How can I recognize and overcome my prejudices in order to help someone in need?

Final Thoughts …

Feasts this Week

July 14	**St Camillus de Lellis (Canada)**
	St Kateri Tekakwitha (USA)
July 15	**St Bonaventure**
July 16	**Our Lady of Mount Carmel**
July 18	**St Camillus de Lellis (USA)**

SUNDAY JULY 20

16th Sunday in Ordinary Time

WHEN I WAS a young bride, we lived in an old Victorian home that really came to life when the dining room was filled with people. My husband was the better cook, so most of the meal preparation was his to do. I specialized in setting a wonderful table with our beautiful wedding gifts. As the years went by, everything became simpler, many wedding gifts gathered dust, and the joy of sharing hospitality at our table with friends and family deepened.

The tradition of welcoming the stranger and the friend at the dinner table runs deep in human history. It is a good thing. We see Abraham engaging the entire household in the rushed preparations to serve unexpected guests. We see Martha bustling about. We see Mary sitting at the feet of Jesus. Then Martha engages Jesus in getting Mary's help with the preparations, and it does not turn out the way she hopes!

Luke does not say how Martha responded. However, we can choose to hear Christ's words spoken not as rebuke, but as a tender invitation to approach more closely, live more deeply, love more richly. Each of us can make the conscious choice to frame today around Jesus Christ, and then we will experience the rest of our world take shape around that choice. Tomorrow we can make the same choice again.

Marilyn Sweet

SUNDAY JULY 20

People and Prayers to Remember this Week

Readings of the Day

Genesis 18.1-10a
Psalm 15

Colossians 1.24-28
Luke 10.38-42

Responding to the Word

Martha and Mary show two ways of being in Christ's presence: one through active service and one through direct attentiveness. Which of these women am I more like? Why?

Final Thoughts ...

Feasts this Week

July 21	**St Lawrence of Brindisi**
July 22	**St Mary Magdalene**
July 23	**St Bridget**
July 24	**St Sharbel Makhluf**
July 25	**St James**
July 26	**St Anne & St Joachim**

SUNDAY JULY 27
World Day of Grandparents and the Elderly

17th Sunday in Ordinary Time

IMAGINE A FATHER and teenage son who rarely speak. They are strangers living under the same roof. For years the father has tried to restore the relationship but the son is always cold, distant, and non-responsive. The sad father longs for things to be the way they used to be.

For some of us, unfortunately, our relationship with God is not so different. This is because we don't pray. Like the son, we sometimes ignore our heavenly father's calls to spend that quality time with him.

Never giving up hope, the father again asks his son if he wants to play catch. Astonishingly, the son agrees. At first it is a bit awkward, but before long they are laughing and really connecting. Afterwards, the son says, "Dad, this was so much fun. We need to do this more often." Unbeknownst to him, his father is holding back tears.

In today's gospel, Jesus invites us to connect (or reconnect) with our heavenly father through prayer. No matter how distant we have been or how far away we have turned, God will rejoice if we respond to his call to spend time with him. He knocks on the door of our hearts every day and waits. Today is the time to let him in. Today is the time to pray!

Connor Brownrigg

SUNDAY JULY 27

People and Prayers to Remember this Week

Readings of the Day

Genesis 18.20-32

Colossians 2.12-14

Psalm 138

Luke 11.1-13

Responding to the Word

Abraham pushes God to greater and greater mercy through his persistent requests on behalf of the innocent. For whom might I ask God's mercy in my prayer today?

Final Thoughts ...

Feasts this Week

July 29	**St Martha, St Mary & St Lazarus**
July 30	**St Peter Chrysologus**
July 31	**St Ignatius of Loyola**
August 1	**St Alphonsus Liguori**
August 2	**St Eusebius of Vercelli**
	St Peter Julian Eymard

SUNDAY AUGUST 3

18th Sunday in Ordinary Time

THE PARABLE OF the rich fool – the man who tore down his barns and built larger ones to store his crops – always reminds me of my parents' teaching on success. They continually reminded my siblings and me that our success would not be measured on earth, but rather in our heavenly home.

No matter what we do in life, whatever our role, education, vocation, titles, responsibilities, or material goods, everything must encourage us to serve our sisters and brothers in need, and ultimately strengthen our relationship with our Creator. When something stands in the way of this call to service and faithfulness, we have a duty to consider whether we are working towards our human potential and revealing the image of God ingrained on each of our souls.

Of course, my folks' teachings are a radical departure from society's definition of success and obsession with material accumulation. Living the Christian life is not for the faint-hearted. Sharing our time, talent, and treasure with each other might deplete our bank accounts and leisure time, but it will ensure we encounter abundance in the life to come.

Unlike the rich fool in today's gospel, may we measure success by our constant service to those in need, and through the growth of our spiritual life and personal relationship with Jesus Christ.

Rev. Matthew Durham, CSB

SUNDAY AUGUST 3

People and Prayers to Remember this Week

Readings of the Day

Ecclesiastes 1.2; 2.21-23
Psalm 90

Colossians 3.1-5, 9-11
Luke 12.13-21

Responding to the Word

The author of Ecclesiastes feels like life passes quickly and often seems meaningless. What has made my life most meaningful?

Final Thoughts …

Feasts this Week

August 4	**St John Mary Vianney**
August 5	**Dedication of the Basilica of St Mary Major**
	Bl Frédéric Janssoone (Canada)
August 6	**Transfiguration of the Lord**
August 7	**St Sixtus II & Companions**
	St Cajetan
August 8	**St Dominic**
August 9	**St Teresa Benedicta of the Cross**

SUNDAY AUGUST 10

19th Sunday in Ordinary Time

For where your treasure is, there your heart will be also.

Don't treasure money: Check. I already know not to focus on wealth. I was feeling pretty pleased with myself, too, until that small voice inside asked: So what, exactly, fills your focus? What's on your mind?

If I'm honest, I'd have to say it's worry. Today, it's my job. Other times I worry about health, finances, or relationships. I just have to watch the news for a world of worries. But everyone worries over things we feel are out of our control. Worry is really the fear of what might happen and we can imagine the worst what-ifs. We play those reels over and over, giving that fear more power, more focus, more energy. Ultimately, we make worry our treasure – like J.R.R. Tolkien's character Gollum and his ring.

I don't *treasure* my worries – that's ridiculous! Is it? Don't those worries take up our thoughts and energy? Aren't they what we talk about most and think about always? Some have even become our stories – a part of how we define ourselves. Sounds like we've made them quite "precious."

Fears are legitimate concerns. It's natural to worry – but it's not productive. If we focus on God, if we bring our fears to him, even the greatest worry can become a powerful prayer.

Caroline Pignat

SUNDAY AUGUST 10

People and Prayers to Remember this Week

Readings of the Day

Wisdom 18.6-9

Hebrews 11.1-2, 8-19

Psalm 33

Luke 12.32-48

Responding to the Word

By faith, we trust that God will give us new life just as God has promised. How have I encouraged others to trust God more fully?

Final Thoughts …

Feasts this Week

August 11	**St Clare**
August 12	**St Jane Frances de Chantal**
August 13	**St Pontian & St Hippolytus**
August 14	**St Maximilian Kolbe**
August 15	**Assumption of the Blessed Virgin Mary**
August 16	**St Stephen of Hungary**

FRIDAY AUGUST 15

Assumption of the Blessed Virgin Mary

A VERY WISE woman once said to me, "In the Magnificat, do you know why the rich are sent away empty? Because they do not have room for God." The proud, the rich, the powerful are already full. There is no room in them for the blessings that come to those who have made room for God in their lives.

The gospel for today tells us about two women who made room for God in their lives. Elizabeth in her old age is pregnant with John the Baptist. She recognizes the presence of God in her own life and in Mary's. Mary, too, chooses to welcome God's gracious love in her life. These women are open, receiving and bringing forth blessings for others.

In today's world, wealth, power, and success are promoted as means to fulfillment. The Magnificat teaches us another way. God chooses the lowly, the weak, and the empty. God is a God of justice, lifting up those who are downtrodden, giving dignity to those who are hungry, poor, or marginalized.

Can we make room for God in our lives, as did Mary and Elizabeth? Can we be open to receive others, to bless them, offer them our abundance, instead of filling ourselves up with empty things? Let us give thanks for God's gracious love, opening us to fulfillment and care for one another.

Beth McIsaac Bruce

FRIDAY AUGUST 15

People and Prayers to Remember this Week

Readings of the Day

Revelation 11.19a; 12.1-6, 10ab
Psalm 45

1 Corinthians 15.20-27
Luke 1.39-56

Responding to the Word

Mary's song of praise says that God has brought down the powerful and filled the hungry with good things. When in my life have I seen God's justice at work?

Final Thoughts …

SUNDAY AUGUST 17

20th Sunday in Ordinary Time

Occasionally the words of Jesus seem to smack us in the face. We shake our heads and move on to something more comforting. Such are the words in today's gospel. Most of us do not want to imagine the possibility of strife and animosity in our family.

Nonetheless, Jesus knew that sometimes families are a hindrance for disciples. In his day, family was often the one structure protecting individuals – but at the cost of a patriarchal system demanding conformity and obedience to authoritarian demands.

In our day, I have seen parents oppose a possible vocation for one of their children, or react negatively when a son or daughter wishes to spend a year working for and with the poor in another country. We also know the pain of parents whose children distance themselves from the faith, despite a good education and faith-filled upbringing.

Choosing the Way of Jesus has never been easy. That is no different today. What Jesus asks of us, however, is that we focus our attention on the true kingdom, that of our Father in heaven, where all are brothers and sisters, especially those most in need. When we work to build God's kingdom, our earthly families can follow along – or go their own way. As painful as that may be for the disciple, the Way is what Jesus demands.

Rev. Mark Miller, CSsR

SUNDAY AUGUST 17

People and Prayers to Remember this Week

Readings of the Day

Jeremiah 38.4-6, 8-10   Hebrews 12.1-4
Psalm 40   Luke 12.49-53

Responding to the Word

Jesus sometimes is the cause of division within families. Has this been the case in my life? If so, how am I called to respond?

Final Thoughts …

Feasts this Week

August 19	**St John Eudes**
August 20	**St Bernard**
August 21	**St Pius X**
August 22	**Queenship of the Blessed Virgin Mary**
August 23	**St Rose of Lima**

SUNDAY AUGUST 24

21st Sunday in Ordinary Time

Ah, the narrow door! A procrastinator by nature, I must confess that today's gospel makes me uncomfortable. Clean up my act, I say to myself, or I'll find myself in that throng, knocking on heaven's door, at risk of joining those who are weeping and gnashing their teeth because they realize that they took for granted all the promise of the kingdom of God.

But just as I am stewing about being ready to enter heaven, I am reminded, "some are last who will be first, and some are first who will be last." With this, my earthly sense of fair play kicks in and I am, yet again, full of righteous indignation that those who seemingly haven't played by the rules are going to bypass the rest of us. So much for my preparedness for passage through that narrow door!

Today we are reminded that we cannot impose earthly rules and expectations on eternal life. God offers all of us passage to the kingdom, but we are required, as St Paul notes, to live a life of discipline – God's discipline. Being loved by God does not mean we won't face trials and pain, but out of our experiences comes the "peaceful fruit of righteousness," the very kind of sustenance that draws people to the banquet in the kingdom of God.

Catherine Mulroney

SUNDAY AUGUST 24

People and Prayers to Remember this Week

Readings of the Day

Isaiah 66.18-21
Psalm 117

Hebrews 12.5-7, 11-13
Luke 13.22-30

Responding to the Word

God gives us the strength to endure our trials. How has God helped me endure my trials?

Final Thoughts ...

Feasts this Week

August 25	**St Louis**
	St Joseph Calasanz
August 27	**St Monica**
August 28	**St Augustine**
August 29	**Passion of St John the Baptist**

SUNDAY AUGUST 31

22nd Sunday in Ordinary Time

Do you remember the time you volunteered at the big parish fundraiser? You threw yourself into the work, sacrificing an enormous amount of your free time, donating generously to help the parish make it a great success. At the parish thank-you dinner, you expected to be seated at the head table but weren't. You *expected* that your efforts would be recognized.

How then should we act? What should be our attitude? Today's first reading and the passage from the Gospel of Luke offer guidance. They speak of the humility we need as Christians, because, as Sirach says, it is only when we are humble that we are truly exalted. Through our humility, the Lord is truly glorified.

Our humility grows from the authenticity of our love and our concern for others. Jesus says everyone who "exalts himself will be humbled, and whoever humbles himself will be exalted." Our proximity to the "head table" in our lives is linked to our invitation to the poor *into* our lives. Pope Francis reminds us we must not place ourselves above others but step down to serve them, especially the poor and vulnerable. As he wrote on Twitter, "To live charitably means not looking out for our own interests, but carrying the burdens of the weakest and poorest among us."

Jack Panozzo

SUNDAY AUGUST 31

People and Prayers to Remember this Week

Readings of the Day

Sirach 3.17-20, 28-29
Psalm 68

Hebrews 12.18-19, 22-24a
Luke 14.1, 7-14

Responding to the Word

Sirach encourages us to be content with our limits and strive to act humbly instead of being arrogant. What tends to make me think more of myself and act in a haughty way toward others?

Final Thoughts ...

Feasts this Week

September 2	**Bl André Grasset (Canada)**
September 3	**St Gregory the Great**
September 4	**Bl Dina Bélanger (Canada)**

SUNDAY SEPTEMBER 7

23rd Sunday in Ordinary Time

I RECENTLY CHATTED with a young woman who had just completed a grueling music examination. She spoke of the long hours spent practicing her repertoire over and over, thinking often about the fun she was missing with her friends. She knew, though, that her focus had to be completely on her music in order to pass her exam.

It's that same kind of focus and dedication that Jesus is talking about in today's gospel when he speaks about hating our loved ones, carrying our crosses, and giving up everything, even our lives. He's telling us to let *nothing* – not even very good things like family and love – get in the way of our willingness to follow him. Our first priority, in everything we do, must be our relationship with Jesus.

If we look at the choices that we make each day, we'll see the many ways we can and do put God first. The construction worker who refuses to use sub-standard materials to cut costs: what's first here, money... or God? The teenager who stands up to the bully, even though she risks being ostracized: what's first here, popularity... or God?

Each time we celebrate the Eucharist, we are given an opportunity to commit ourselves once again to putting God first in our lives. May our Amen resound with the strength of our commitment!

Teresa Whalen Lux

SUNDAY SEPTEMBER 7

People and Prayers to Remember this Week

Readings of the Day

Wisdom 9.13-18
Psalm 90

Philemon 9-10, 12-17
Luke 14.25-33

Responding to the Word

Without God's help, our minds, no matter how sharp, always fall short of understanding God's ways and plans. What help do I most need from God today?

Final Thoughts ...

Feasts this Week

September 8	**Nativity of the Blessed Virgin Mary**
September 9	**St Peter Claver**
September 12	**Most Holy Name of Mary**
September 13	**St John Chrysostom**

SUNDAY SEPTEMBER 14

The Exaltation of the Holy Cross

AT THE ROOT of all violence and destruction in the world is the human need to control. We want so much to be like God, to be God, that we push the limits of power and step on each other in the process. Isn't it ironic, then, that the only human being who could ever legitimately claim equality with God was the very one who let go of that claim?

Jesus, the Son of Man, emptied himself of all divine power and gave himself over to death on a cross. In surrendering the advantage of his own divine nature, he won for us a share in that very nature. In giving up the use of worldly power, he showed us a new way of seeing the power found in humility and service to others. This is the feast we celebrate today, the victory of love over hatred, the triumph of life over death.

Jesus, the Word Made Flesh, revealed to us the unimaginable depth and breadth of God's love, given to us that we may have eternal life. The triumph of the cross is a powerful invitation to each one of us to unite ourselves with Christ in the mystery of the eucharistic celebration and claim a new kind of victory won for us by the death and resurrection of Love Incarnate.

Sr. Mary Ellen Green, OP

SUNDAY SEPTEMBER 14

People and Prayers to Remember this Week

Readings of the Day

Numbers 21.4-9
Psalm 78

Philippians 2.6-11
John 3.13-17

Responding to the Word

Jesus, even though he was God, humbled himself to the point of death. Which part of my life is God calling me to a greater humility at this time?

Final Thoughts ...

Feasts this Week

September 15	**Our Lady of Sorrows**
September 16	**St Cornelius & St Cyprian**
September 17	**St Robert Bellarmine**
	St Hildegard of Bingen
September 19	**St Januarius**
September 20	**St Andrew Kim Tae-gŏn, Paul Chŏng Ha-sang & Companions**

SUNDAY SEPTEMBER 21

25th Sunday in Ordinary Time

In Tanzania, within sight of Mount Kilimanjaro, the local church runs an experimental farm. They have little to work with other than their grit and determination. More often than not, what sees them through is their ingenuity. Can't afford a replacement part? Make the part. Don't have a lathe to fabricate it? Figure out how to construct one from the scraps on hand. They continue to try to improve the lives of the local people in this East African country. This is a tough struggle on an average annual wage of around $1,200 per person.

Maybe it is this kind of ingenuity that Luke points to in the parable of the unjust manager in today's gospel. What if we used our ingenuity even half as well as the unjust steward? How far could we go towards promoting the kingdom of God by righting unjust trading systems or seeking a fair distribution of resources for all? What could be done about the dramatically widening gap between rich and poor?

Let us put our ingenuity and other talents at the service of our brothers and sisters, in the image of our Lord who "raises the poor from the dust and lifts the needy from the ash heap." Let us strive always to put people first.

Michael Dougherty

SUNDAY SEPTEMBER 21

People and Prayers to Remember this Week

Readings of the Day

Amos 8.4-7　　　　　　　　1 Timothy 2.1-8
Psalm 113　　　　　　　　　Luke 16.1-13

Responding to the Word

Paul encourages us to pray for those in authority. What prayers do I want to offer for leaders in the Church and in the state?

Final Thoughts ...

Feasts this Week

September 23	St Pius of Pietrelcina
September 24	Bl Émilie Tavernier-Gamelin (Canada)
September 25	St Cosmas & St Damian (Canada)
September 26	St John de Brébeuf, St Isaac Jogues & Companions (Canada)
	St Cosmas & St Damian (USA)
September 27	St Vincent de Paul

SUNDAY SEPTEMBER 28
World Day of Migrants and Refugees

26th Sunday in Ordinary Time

ONE DAY A catechist told the parable of Lazarus and the rich man to her class. As she spoke, she was tying knots in a beautiful scarf. "Each knot is for a time when we close our hearts to those who are like Lazarus," she said. "Who is like Lazarus?" a child asked. "Lazarus is everywhere," she replied. "He is all the hungry people who wait for crumbs from our table. He is those suffering from natural disasters and war. He is the addict and the abused. He is our neighbor."

"Who is the rich man?" another queried. Continuing to tie knots, the catechist responded, "The rich man is everywhere, too. He is those who never share their wealth with the poor, who ignore sorrow and suffering, who are selfish with time and concern." The scarf grew shorter; soon, it was a tight ball, no longer useful or beautiful. The catechist continued, "When we close hearts to those in need, we end up like the rich man: with a withered heart, tight and useless like this knotted scarf. That is the greatest poverty of all."

At this time of harvest bounty, and goodness of life, the readings shake us out of our complacency and call us to radical conversion. They call us to open our hearts generously and close the chasm that exists between the rich and the poor.

Wanda Conway

SUNDAY SEPTEMBER 28

People and Prayers to Remember this Week

Readings of the Day

Amos 6.1a, 4-7
Psalm 146

1 Timothy 6.11-16
Luke 16.19-31

Responding to the Word

The rich man never noticed the poor and starving Lazarus right at his gate. What can I do to not just notice but to actually help the poor and homeless who come into my life?

Final Thoughts ...

Feasts this Week

September 29	**St Michael, St Gabriel & St Raphael**
September 30	**St Jerome**
October 1	**St Thérèse of the Child Jesus**
October 2	**Holy Guardian Angels**
October 4	**St Francis of Assisi**

SUNDAY OCTOBER 5

27th Sunday in Ordinary Time

SHEEP, TO MY mind, live in a kind of gated community. They are kept together not so much by physical barriers as by the special care of the shepherd who enfolds the flock within a powerful, if figurative, protective fence.

The People of God are often described as God's sheep. For Christians, the door into the sheepfold is Christ. Entering the fold by emptying ourselves, we gladly accept our dependence upon God because we have witnessed the constant and loving care of the shepherd in countless saving deeds.

Once in a while, however, we sheep wonder if we cannot seek greener pastures on our own. Israel, grumbling in the wilderness, wondered if it might not have been better off going it alone. Sometimes all of us, like Timothy, lose heart, become ashamed and fearful of preaching the gospel, wallow in self-pity, and water down the truth.

Jesus both chides and encourages us – even a minimal amount of true faith in him will be enough to do what God requires of us. We are thankful today for God' generosity and for God's grace poured out freely on us, through no merit of our own. We bask in the abundant loving care of God, adopting in return a humble, constant, and faith-filled stance towards our maker.

Christine Mader

SUNDAY OCTOBER 5

People and Prayers to Remember this Week

Readings of the Day

Habakkuk 1.2-3; 2.2-4
Psalm 95

2 Timothy 1.6-8, 13-14
Luke 17.5-10

Responding to the Word

Habakkuk yearns for justice amid the violence and strife of his world. How can I join with others to help overcome the violence and injustice that permeate our society today?

Final Thoughts …

Feasts this Week

October 6	**Bl Marie-Rose Durocher**
	St Bruno
October 7	**Our Lady of the Rosary**
October 9	**St Denis & Companions**
	St John Leonardi
October 11	**St John XXIII**

SUNDAY OCTOBER 12

28th Sunday in Ordinary Time

THERE ARE A lot of "peripheries" in today's gospel. Pope Francis often uses the word to translate the margins of society to which he urges us to take Christ's compassion. Jesus was going through the region between Samaria and Galilee, whose populations of Samaritans and Jews were usually bitter enemies. Such frontiers were fraught with ethnic and religious tensions.

Lepers were also people of the "periphery," living on the edges of communities, isolated for fear of contagion. Their disease had allied ancient enemies who knew one thing. The Master who approached did not fear those on the margins, and indiscriminately lavished God's mercy and healing on them. The lepers asked for mercy. Jesus offered it, and then wondered at the gratitude expressed by only one – the hated Samaritan. To all, Jesus had given life: he had re-created, healed, and restored them to family, friends, community.

Jesus offers life restored to us too. Perhaps we imagine ourselves far from the margins, little in need of mercy. But in moments of utter honesty, we recognize that we too are marginalized. We need healing. Jesus invites us to trust his word of power, and to surrender ourselves to God to be transformed and restored by his Spirit in the Eucharist so that, brimming with gratitude and joy, we may return to the margins as bearers of God's mercy.

Bernadette Gasslein

SUNDAY OCTOBER 12

People and Prayers to Remember this Week

Readings of the Day

2 Kings 5.14-17
Psalm 98

2 Timothy 2.8-13
Luke 17.11-19

Responding to the Word

Jesus wonders why those healed do not express thanks. When have I failed to express my thanks for what God has done for me?

Final Thoughts ...

Feasts this Week

October 13	Thanksgiving Day (Canada)
October 14	St Callistus I
October 15	St Teresa of Jesus
October 16	St Marguerite d'Youville (Canada)
	St Hedwig (USA)
	St Margaret Mary Alacoque (USA)
October 17	St Ignatius of Antioch
October 18	St Luke

SUNDAY OCTOBER 19
World Mission Sunday

29th Sunday in Ordinary Time

IN TODAY'S GOSPEL, we hear Jesus teach his disciples to be persistent in prayer. Far too often, we are discouraged when a prayer seems to go unanswered. We might question whether it is worth repeating our plea and feelings of desperation may arise. However, the gospel – the parable of the determined widow and the stubborn judge – reminds us of the importance of being resolute in our prayer life.

Persistence in prayer is an act of confidence and discipline of the soul that strengthens our relationship with God. It's the subtle understanding and humble acceptance that God's will is perfect and that his answer will be given at the right time. His time. Thus, we ought to hope and wait in him. We need that time to comprehend what God is allowing us to experience. Through persistence in prayer, we are encouraged to partake in a communication of love, praise, and trust.

In fact, there is no such thing as an unanswered prayer. There are, perhaps, unexpected answers to our prayers. These answers will always be better than what we could ever expect. After all, we are not pleading with a dishonest judge but with God who loves utterly. Keep praying, keep believing, keep hoping: he is already working in your life, in one way or the other. He answers your prayers; the Lord is faithful.

Monica Nino

SUNDAY OCTOBER 19

People and Prayers to Remember this Week

Readings of the Day

Exodus 17.8-13　　　　　　　　2 Timothy 3.14 – 4.2
Psalm 121　　　　　　　　　　Luke 18.1-8

Responding to the Word

Jesus wants us to be persistent in our prayer. For what do I continually ask God for myself? For others?

Final Thoughts ...

Feasts this Week

October 20	St Hedwig (Canada)
	St Margaret Mary Alacoque (Canada)
	St Paul of the Cross (USA)
October 22	St John Paul II
	Anniversary of Dedication of Churches whose date of consecration is unknown (Canada)
October 23	St John of Capistrano
October 24	St Anthony Mary Claret

SUNDAY OCTOBER 26

30th Sunday in Ordinary Time

As a child, I grew up not far from a seminary and was always enthralled by the stories of missionaries. It seemed like an incredible calling to go to distant places like China or the North and dedicate your life to a higher cause. But what a shocking gospel story to read today: Jesus criticizes the religious leader while the sinner is praised! Can that be an appropriate attitude for Christians?

The permanent temptation for those of us who reside in the wealthy parts of the globe may well be to become like the Pharisee, described as someone full of conceit and contempt for others. A true missioner knows that a domineering attitude, lack of empathy, and a dearth of humility are far from being religious attributes. No matter how often we go to church or how much we place in the collection basket, this parable cautions us never to view others with self-righteous disdain. Rather, we are called to pour our energies out as a libation of solidarity, mercy, and justice.

We are all called to be disciples whose service is pleasing to the Lord, so that our prayer will be accepted and reach to the clouds. When we recognize that God listens to the prayer of the person who is wronged, we understand that humble sinners can also become great missionaries.

Joe Gunn

SUNDAY OCTOBER 26

People and Prayers to Remember this Week

Readings of the Day

Sirach 35.15-17, 20-22 (Canada)
Sirach 35.12-14, 16-18 (USA)
Psalm 34

2 Timothy 4.6-8, 16-18
Luke 18.9-14

Responding to the Word

God hears the cries of the oppressed, and we must help to root out injustice. What can I do today to help change little injustices that are found in my household, my workplace, or my neighborhood?

Final Thoughts …

Feasts this Week

October 28   **St Simon & St Jude**
November 1   **All Saints**

SUNDAY NOVEMBER 2
The Commemoration of All the Faithful Departed

All Souls' Day

SHE WAS NINE years old and had never known her grandparents. Three had died before she was born but she was vaguely aware of one grandmother who lived in Eastern Europe. One day, a letter arrived for her father. When he opened it, it bore the news that his mother had died. He wept and she wept with him. The visible grief displayed by a father who never cried joined her both to the family that she knew and loved and to the generations that had gone before her. And in her nine-year-old way, she grieved and began to gather and keep wonderful memories of the grandparents she never knew.

The feast of All Souls celebrates that we are all, past and present, connected in Christ. Today we reflect on our ancestors who already feast at the messianic banquet; we remember that the grain of wheat must die so that life may continue in all its richness. We reflect on Jesus, who, by his cross and resurrection, vanquished sin and death once, for all. As Christians, we know that death has no hold over us, and that through our own cross and death we too shall live forever. Today, we who still wait are one with those who already feast at the heavenly banquet.

Wanda Conway

SUNDAY NOVEMBER 2

People and Prayers to Remember this Week

Readings of the Day

*other readings may be chosen

Wisdom 3.1-9
Psalm 116

Revelation 21.1-5a, 6b-7
Luke 7.11-17

Responding to the Word

Wisdom reflects on the destiny of the righteous people. How can I prioritize quality of life over quantity of life?

Final Thoughts …

Feasts this Week

November 3   **St Martin de Porres**
November 4   **St Charles Borromeo**

SUNDAY NOVEMBER 9

The Dedication of the Lateran Basilica

DEDICATIONS OF CHURCHES have become a rarity lately. We rather hear about dioceses merging, parishes closing, or even churches being put up for sale. Given such a context, a feast like the Dedication of the Lateran Basilica in Rome is not likely to appeal much even to those who still come to church on Sundays.

Yet today's readings supply insights about places of worship that are worth pondering. Both the first reading and the gospel acknowledge the beauty and the importance of a sacred place like the Jerusalem Temple. They remind us as well that life given by God cannot be confined, even to a building, be it the most revered temple or sanctuary.

Jesus and his disciples had great respect for the Temple, but Jesus warns us against giving too much importance to anything built of human hands. God's presence cannot be contained in one particular building. More and better than in any temple, God's presence has now been made manifest in all of Jesus' life among us and will endure forever through his resurrection.

But that's not the end of the story. We too, by having a share in the resurrection of Christ, have become sacred places where God and the Spirit wish to dwell. May we allow them to abide in us so that people around us will recognize God's presence in our lives.

Jean-Pierre Prévost

SUNDAY NOVEMBER 9

People and Prayers to Remember this Week

Readings of the Day

Ezekiel 47.1-2, 8-9, 12
Psalm 46

1 Corinthians 3.9b-11, 16-17
John 2.13-22

Responding to the Word

Paul reminds us that we are God's temple and God's Spirit dwells within us. How can I treat my human body with more respect and integrity?

Final Thoughts ...

Feasts this Week

November 10	**St Leo the Great**
November 11	**St Martin of Tours**
November 12	**St Josaphat**
November 13	**St Frances Xavier Cabrini (USA)**
November 15	**St Albert the Great**

SUNDAY NOVEMBER 16
World Day of the Poor

33rd Sunday in Ordinary Time

Today's scripture texts offer encouragement for the faithful who worship God and try to live justly and righteously. Because it sometimes seems that those who live for themselves alone appear to thrive, such good news is timely.

The community Malachi addresses found it difficult to distinguish right from wrong, since the faithless seemed to trump the faithful every time. When they wondered whether serving God was worth it, Malachi insisted that clear lines would eventually be drawn between evil and good, evildoers and the righteous. The righteous could look forward to vindication, healing, and the warmth of God's faithful love towards them.

A different kind of encouragement is afforded to the Christian community at Thessalonika. Long-suffering in their care of indolent members perfectly capable of looking after themselves but too busy prying into others' affairs to work, these faithful Christians are released from supporting and socializing with those who were giving the community a bad name.

Finally, as we wait for the Lord's return in glory, Christians can depend on the indwelling presence of God's Holy Spirit for assistance. With this assurance, we need not be concerned about exact dates and times, but only with fidelity and constancy in our discipleship.

Christine Mader

SUNDAY NOVEMBER 16

People and Prayers to Remember this Week

Readings of the Day

Malachi 3.19-20a (USA)
Malachi 4.1-2 (Canada)
Psalm 98

2 Thessalonians 3.7-12
Luke 21.5-19

Responding to the Word

Jesus promises that amid trials and difficulties he will give us wisdom in speaking our witness to him. When have I been given just the right words to offer some needed help to others?

Final Thoughts ...

Feasts this Week

November 17	St Elizabeth of Hungary
November 18	Dedication of the Basilicas of St Peter & St Paul
	St Rose Philippine Duchesne (USA)
November 21	Presentation of the Blessed Virgin Mary
November 22	St Cecilia

SUNDAY NOVEMBER 23
World Day of Youth

Our Lord Jesus Christ, King of the Universe

EARLY IN HIS papacy, Pope Francis used a striking image to describe the kind of leadership priests should exercise in their faith communities. He urged them to be shepherds marked by "the smell of the sheep." A similar image appears in today's first reading, where God names King David as the "shepherd of my people Israel." The reading from Colossians describes the supreme authority of Christ over all things. Yet throughout his earthly ministry, Jesus modeled servant leadership, which we could also call "shepherd leadership."

The daily news often shows a different style of leadership, characterized by arrogance, greed, hunger for power, and a disregard for the common good. The kind of leadership suggested in today's readings, by contrast, is marked by service, humility, and compassion. As the taunting onlookers in the gospel scene mock the kingship of Jesus, we get a glimpse into the heart of true leadership. In the interaction between the crucified Jesus and the "good thief," we see an example of a humble petitioner – "Jesus, remember me" – receiving not judgment, but forgiveness: "Today you will be with me in Paradise."

Today we seek the grace to practice and to encourage, through our prayers and our actions, the kind of shepherd leadership modeled by Jesus.

Krystyna Higgins

SUNDAY NOVEMBER 23

People and Prayers to Remember this Week

Readings of the Day

2 Samuel 5.1-3
Psalm 122

Colossians 1.12-20
Luke 23.35-43

Responding to the Word

God has brought us into Christ's kingdom community. How can I thank God for this wonderful gift?

Final Thoughts …

Feasts this Week

November 24	**St Andrew Dũng-Lạc & Companions**
November 25	**St Catherine of Alexandria**
November 27	**Thanksgiving Day (USA)**

My Spiritual Journey

♥Living with Christ Canada's companion
to praying and living the Eucharist

Come home to faith!
Each issue includes:

- Complete Scripture readings for every day of the week
- All the prayers of the Mass
- Reflections for Sundays and feast day liturgies
- Suggested forms of the Prayer of the Faithful
- Saints' bios and inspirational quotes

14 issues (monthly + special Christmas and Easter issues)

Get the PLUS!
Daily reflections for ADVENT and LENT!

CANADIAN EDITION
To subscribe: visit **en.novalis.ca** or call **1 800 387-7164**

♥Living with Christ Your Daily Companion
for Praying and Living the Eucharist

For today's American Catholic
Each issue includes:

- 12 monthly issues including Holy Week
- Full liturgical texts for daily and Sunday Masses
- Insights on the spiritual life from best-selling authors
- Brief reflections on the Sunday and daily readings
- Follows the American liturgical calendar, as set by the USCCB

Get the PLUS!
Daily reflections for ADVENT and LENT!

AMERICAN EDITION
To subscribe, call **1 800 214-3386** (mention code **S2509PJ**)
or visit us at **livingwithchrist.us**